is 65 the new 25?

...reclaiming your life;

becoming who you were meant to be

by
donna m. bennett

is 65 the new 25?
...reclaiming your life; becoming who you were meant to be

First Printing January 2014
Copyright © 2014 Donna M. Bennett

ISBN–13: 978-1493526673
ISBN–10: 1493526677

ACKNOWLEDGMENT FOR PERMISSION
TO REPRINT THE FOLLOWING:

Quote from the book, *Letters to a Young Poet,* Copyright © 2000 by
Rainer Maria Rilke. Reprinted with permission of New World Library,
Novato, CA. www.newworldlibrary.com.

Quote from the book, *Let Your Life Speak, Listening for the Voice of
Vocation,* by Parker Palmer, Copyright © 2000 by John Wiley & Sons, Inc.
This material is reproduced with permission of John Wiley & Sons, Inc.

Quote from the book, *Finding Meaning in the Second Half of Life:
How to Finally, Really Grow Up,* by James Hollis, Ph.D.
Copyright © 2005, published by Gotham Books,
a division of Penguin Group (USA), Inc. Permission granted by the author.

Print copies available at http://createspace.com
Printed by CreateSpace, An Amazon.com Company
Email: bennettdonna446@gmail.com
Website: www.donnambennett.com

Cover and book design: Janson Graphics LLC
jansongraphics.com

Also by Donna M. Bennett

When You Lose Your Job

Expressions of the Heart

(Quotes compiled by Barbara Laporte,

illustrated by Donna M. Bennett)

I dedicate this book to

Andrea (Andy) Gilats who when she retired,

left a legacy of applied learning,

beauty, creativity and imagination,

and who continues this legacy

in her post-career life, living and giving her talents

to enrich the lives of others.

Introduction

Once upon a generation ago, retirement was a clearly defined stage of transition that happened sometime between the ages of 55 and 65. There was no 'how to' since people followed the cultural way, which was to stop working and to spend their days in some leisurely fashion.

Today we are offered a palette of options for our retirement. With it comes the uncertainty of how to continue our usefulness in this time of greater longevity. We also have the opportunity for self-discovery, exploring and trying new things that complete who we started out to be. Adulthood for the boomer generation was all about responsibility, duty, loyalty, and lock-step focus. Individuality, personal dreams, and budding talents were moved to a shelf labeled 'someday', as 'I' became 'we' and eventually - 'us'.

In this book, I offer my best advice, guidance, and counsel for your transition in this new age of retirement. I ask only that you take from these essays that which makes the most sense for you and your life, and apply it to achieve your greatest fulfillment.

**Ask the questions
∼ let the answers evolve**

The essays in this book are guides to help you make choices for your fullest life, whether in transition to, or in the midst of living your post-career life.

As you read the essays, keep these questions in mind, and apply the guides as they fit for your life.

Intention
1. Who am I?
2. How do I want to spend my time?
   And with whom?
3. Where do I want to live?
4. What is in my control?
5. What is most important to me?
6. What do I want to learn?
7. What skills/talents do I want to develop
   or further develop?

Action
O What actions will I take to fulfill my intention?

Barriers
O What will get in my way, and how will I prepare
   for these barriers knowing they will pop up?

Support
O Who is the person(s) I trust most to support
   me in my choices/decisions to create a quality of
   life that is right for me?

Becoming...

(in the philosophy of Aristotle)
any change from the lower level of
potentiality to the higher level of actuality.

World English Dictionary

Contents

Change & Transition

*The period of change and transition
from career into post-career life is one that
impacts each of us in different ways.
The degree of its impact largely depends on
the current state of our lives,
our past experience with change, our personality,
and the number of unknowns that lie ahead.*

*The following essays are meant to
help build an awareness
of your personal process through change,
to guide you through a proactive,
intentional approach, and to offer suggestions
to help you on the way.*

3

1

...*first we mourn*

Loss is inherent in the human experience, and a constant in all of life. Yet, when it happens, we are often surprised – as if it had never happened before. As if it isn't *supposed* to happen. And loss often comes all wrapped up in negatives - negative thoughts, words, and emotions.

I asked several people: "What words bubble up when you think of loss?" They were quick to respond with words such as: regret, uncertainty, grief, sorrow, emptiness, missing, overwhelmed, anger, isolation, separation, sadness, pain, alone, stalled; one person offered: "release, hope, and joy".

All had experienced current or recent losses such as job loss, career change, a parent's health, children leaving the nest, personal health issues, and the loss of someone close. Some losses were expected, and some came as a shock. It doesn't seem to matter. Expected or not, loss and the effects of loss contain an element of surprise.

When loss is a matter of choice, such as leaving a job or career that no longer fits, or leaving a hurtful relationship, relocating, or retiring, there are still surprises, as the relief of leaving may be followed by anxiety and fear of the unknown.

While loss is inherent in human experience, many find a need to move quickly away from it. Others choose to hang on to what was, literally and/or emotionally, because the unknown - the place beyond the loss - is too difficult to imagine.

As surprise is found in loss, it is also found in gain. As you open yourself to new possibilities, and prepare to take action in a new direction, surprise will surface again as you discover that fear and anxiety diminish as you are empowered by taking action.

For example, in the case of job loss, career change, or retirement, self-discovery is often a by-product of loss. It is filled with surprise as you rediscover strengths and talents that, in the past, may have been unutilized or underutilized, and are now valued in a new field or endeavor.

It can be difficult to imagine gain after loss. Emotions tend to take all the space reserved for energy or new ideas. It often takes some thing, or some one, outside of ourselves to get us moving again (i.e., a counselor, a class, a support group, a friend).

Whether planned or unplanned, expected or unexpected, it is critical to our emotional health to mourn our losses. That is, to feel them, experience them, talk about them, celebrate what was, and celebrate what will be. If not properly mourned, our losses will go underground and attach to the next loss, compounding the impact of new loss.

What is common in loss is:

…what once was, will never be again, and what is to come, will be new and different.

So first, we must mourn, and prepare for transition to what is next. One way to prepare is to make a list

6

of what you must say good-bye to (both the good and the bad) and another list of what you can say hello to. I have found this to be a profound exercise with many people I have counseled and coached through loss. What becomes possible in this exercise is – HOPE.

2

Ascending the Ladder of Personal Needs

Life and transition are inseparable. Most transitions are accompanied by some degree of loss. The greater the loss, the more one's focus shifts from higher order human needs (meaning and potential) to a lower order of human needs (food, shelter, security).

The order of human needs is based on psychologist Abraham Maslow's well-known theory and model: *Hierarchy of Human Needs* (Maslow's 1943 paper, "A Theory of Human Motivation"). Maslow proposed that our basic requirements must be filled in order to focus on our higher order needs. Maslow describes his *Hierarchy of Human Needs* in this order:

1. Physiological (e.g., food, shelter, water, air)
2. Safety and Security (e.g., personal and financial)

3. Love and Belonging (e.g., family, friends, intimacy)

4. Esteem (e.g., acceptance, achievement, and respect)

5. Self-actualization (e.g., meaning and potential)

When our basic, fundamental needs are threatened, it is likely that the pursuit of our higher order needs will be abandoned. Fulfilling basic need, according to Maslow, will always be necessary to the foundation of one's quality of life.

Transitions that are likely to cause a threat to basic needs include loss of a close relationship, health issues, job loss, divorce, or unfulfilled dreams and goals.

Retirement, and the time leading up to it, also belongs in the category of transition and loss. The time between ages 55 and 75 – what some have called our 'third age', is one of the most impactful transitions. Each person will enter it on terms that have been defined by the 'first' and 'second' stages of their lives.

How are you managing this transition? Where do you find yourself in Maslow's Hierarchy?

You may be leaning toward retirement, or seeking a different kind of work, or a combination of both. These decisions involve a loss and an ending of what has been known, and is often accompanied by fear of what is unknown.

If it's time to be thinking about your post-career life, yet you feel stuck and indecisive, take a measure of your circumstances. Are your needs being met on levels 1, 2, and 3? Are you recovering from a loss or loss upon loss? Or, have you recovered and are not yet ready to pursue your greater potential and purpose?

Wherever you find yourself, and whatever must work itself out, focus on what you are able to do, and the resources and support you need to get back on solid ground. Put your time and energy there. It's important to understand that things will not be the same as before. This takes acceptance in order to take the next steps.

When you feel reassured that you have done what you can to satisfy your basic needs, you will once again find the energy to focus on accomplishing your higher level needs – esteem, meaning and potential.

11

3

Grit & Gratitude

Thresholds, transitions, and transformations all represent unknowns, and can fill us with a sense of powerlessness. Particularly, when we find ourselves in completely uncharted territory such as post-career life. Powerlessness calls for acts of courage, strength, trust, and tenacity - a time for true grit!

Life beyond career used to be all mapped out. We merely followed those who went before – parents, grandparents, and great-grandparents. As a society, we ended our careers by stepping out of one way of life and into another. Like it or not, the majority followed the societal course. They left work behind, and replaced it with leisure. It was the way to retire.

Society, however, is shifting and changing in the wake of Baby Boomers. As Boomers have changed the course of society in each stage of their human development, they also demand a new way to 'retire'. The old model no longer works. Careers are phased out, rather than ended, and people now look for ways to recycle their personal gifts and resources.

The new retirement has no set rules and is identified by new names or phrases that are a better fit such as, 'encore careers', the 'second half of life', and similar versions. With no rules or precedence to guide us, we must create our own way. We now have more options. We can do what we want with the rest of our lives. Where to begin?

In the process of transition, we are likely to focus on external resources and overlook internal resources; resources such as the powerful emotion of giving gratitude. Feeling rudderless, filled with doubt and fear, it is typical to focus on things outside of our selves and forget to look within. Giving gratitude is one way to do that. It can help you refocus, work out some of the stress, and see things in a new light.

To get in touch with gratitude, create a list by taking a look back at your career, your activities, and your relationships. Uncover the places for gratitude. This can be both a humbling and a rewarding experience. Open a journal or notebook and create your list by answering the following questions:

- O What has worked in the past?
- O What were your successes, your accomplishments?
- O What gave you energy and a feeling of purpose and worth?
- O Who did you learn from? Who learned from you? How was that learning applied?
- O How did you recover from setbacks, disappointments, and change?
- O What processes did you follow that worked well for you?
- O What were you proud of?
- O Where did you receive support?
- O What surprised you about yourself?
- O What do you do naturally that serves as a strength?
- O If you were to ask 5 people across the spectrum of your life, what strengths would they attribute to you? (If you're unsure, ask them).

When on a new course, doubts and fears can knock you off track. Your gratitude list can give you the grit to stay focused.

4

Resistance, Revelation, Resilience

Resistance *(refusal to accept something new or different, Merriam-Webster, m-w.com)*

Personal growth comes in many shapes and sizes, and always with some degree of change.

Whether invited, expected, or imposed, change is not only inevitable in the process of growth, but it is often followed by feelings of uncertainty and doubt. Those feelings are heightened when a sense of control begins to slip away. One way we try to stop the slippage is to put on the armor of resistance.

The amount of resistance usually depends on the impact of the change. Some resistance can help put things in perspective as it helps us to slow down and evaluate our circumstances. Resistance can also paralyze us from

16

taking any action.

That is the point when going back is impossible, and going forward is unimaginable. When no matter which way you turn, fear, panic, and worry hold you back. **Fear** of all the unknowns, and **panic** created by that inner voice that shouts, "What if I fail? And by the dire warnings of others, "You're going to try WHAT?"

It can feel so scary that staying in place seems more comfortable than taking even one small step forward. You see no options, nothing feels right, and you are stuck. It's okay and healthy to be stuck for a while if the time is used productively. If not, and you stay stuck too long, you may find yourself in a permanent, rather than situational, state of resistance.

So, how can you get yourself unstuck and moving again? You don't suddenly discard the unsettled feelings. That's unrealistic. Rather, you can choose to take fear, panic and worry along with you. Then watch how they get smaller the more you take action and regain control of your choices and decisions.

Revelation *(a pleasant often enlightening surprise, Merriam-Webster, m-w.com)*

The goal then is to make a fluid transition from resistance to revelation. To do that, make an honest analysis of what holds you back. Then, without self-judgment or defensiveness, take note of your choices. You can choose to stay frozen in self-doubts and fears, or you can make the transition a productive, imaginative, and active time of growth and discovery. How? Begin by using every trusted resource available to you (friends, classes, colleagues, mentors, internet, acquaintances) - any one or any thing that informs and increases your knowledge towards positivity and action. This has a wonderful side effect: it gets you back in control of your own life.

18

Resilience *(an ability to recover from or adjust easily to misfortune or change, Merriam-Webster, m-w.com)*

When you shed the armor of resistance and open yourself to revelation, you allow a flow of resilience. Resilience is when you have learned to move with and beyond challenges until it becomes a part of you. So that, when you come to another stage of personal growth, you can tap into your past experience with change, and choose resilience to move forward again. Rather than 'learned helplessness', you learn to take control, and create and manage each new stage of life. Things won't be the same. They will be different at every juncture. Yet each time it will be growth and change that you can personally claim as your own.

5

CHANGE:
Step back, Step in, Step out

Life begins with change. The newborn leaves the safety
and familiarity of the womb to begin its life and its first
encounter with a lifetime cycle of endings and beginnings.
These are the vulnerable places that call for preparation
for what is new, and closure of what is left behind. In time,
the newborn will have the ability of choice and personal
history to guide him and her through these cycles.

When change occurs out of tragedy or deep personal
loss, closure is not about forgetting; it is about continuing
to live, and allowing all that is needed in order to move
on. There are many places where change occurs during
our life cycles. To move on, it will always be necessary
to put closure to the ending and prepare for the new
beginning. The time it takes in this process will depend

on how deeply you are impacted.

As you enter these new places, it is typical to feel a combination of both fear and excitement. Something has ended, something new is beginning and a wall of unknowns, options, and decisions must be moved through.

A period of adjustment will be needed until moving forward can no longer be avoided. At that point, you have the choice to respond passively, reactively, or pro-actively; it is up to you. A passive or reactive response - often driven by fear – can either stop you in your tracks, or force you to jump too quickly. A proactive approach or response will give you the greatest feeling of control, helping you contain and ease your fear.

To act proactively, begin by breathing deeply, then give yourself time to take this 3-step approach to managing change: ***step back, step in and step out.***

STEP BACK ***(ask yourself some questions)***

- Will my choices/decisions/actions have an impact on those close to me (i.e., financially, emotionally, time-related)? How and to what extent?

- ♂ What are my typical behaviors/responses when faced with change?
- ♂ Have I fully put closure to what is ending before preparing for and moving into the new beginning?
- ♂ When I look at ways in which I have handled change in the past, did my actions work well, not so well, or not at all? If I want to change my actions, how will I make that happen (what do I want to **stop, start, continue**)?
- ♂ Have I identified resources that may be helpful? Have I thoroughly explored and/or utilized those resources?

STEP IN *(reflect on your answers; take action as necessary)*

- ♂ Communicate (with those close to you)
- ♂ Become informed (classes, books, networks, mentors)
- ♂ Explore (ideas, opportunities, possibilities)

O Get support (ask a trusted friend to lend a listening/non-judging ear; and/or turn to a coach who has expertise in helping people through transitions)

STEP OUT

O Set manageable goals

O Take appropriate action

O Identify and plan for barriers

23

Change and transition are part of a cyclical life pattern; they will come both unexpectedly and inevitably. You get to respond the way that works best for you and your life. The opportunity is yours.

6

Relationships & Change

Relationships are most vulnerable in times of change and transition. Yet when we are in the confusion and uncertainty of change, the impact on those closest to us is often overlooked.

Not because we plan it that way, but because we are human! Faced with change, whether expected or unexpected, imposed or self-imposed, there is a process that begins with our initial reaction followed by a period of adjustment to a new phase. It is typical to be self-focused at these junctures.

Change and transition are often thought to be interchangeable. However, according to William Bridges (1991), they are two different things - one set in motion by the other. Change is situational and external - something has ended or stopped, and will never again be the

24

same. In contrast, the effect from the change happens internally or emotionally, creating a period of adjustment and transition. The time it takes to adjust depends on the change, how deeply it impacts us, and how we respond. It is important then, to note the loss inherent in change, before readying ourselves for a new beginning. Understanding this process can be very validating if the effects of change continue to linger.

As we adjust and begin to move forward, we have choices and decisions to make. This is the time to go slowly and to prepare and plan for life after change.

During this phase, it is critical to communicate our feelings, thoughts, and desires to others who are also impacted - our partners, wives, husbands, and possibly other family members. Again, it is human nature to focus on our own uncertainty, not wanting to burden others. As a result, it is likely that we will assume that others understand what we're going through. Failing to communicate, especially at such pivotal times, can create problems for couples and families. Misunderstandings and misconceptions left unspoken and unclarified can lead to longer-term rifts in relationships.

Retirement is an especially vulnerable time for relationships. Change and transition are what retirement is all about. Our needs and our quality of life (how we want to spend our time, money and talents) are on the line. And each person in the relationship is likely to have different needs and ideas about retirement.

So, no matter how awkward or difficult - have the conversation. For couples, it helps if you each list and describe what it means to have a quality of life in retirement. Include all that is relative, such as finances, friendships, family, leisure, learning, travel, health, residence, etc. Then compare notes. If you are poles apart in the areas where your lives intersect, try finding a place of collaboration, as opposed to compromise.

Having the conversation is what is important. Even if you find it difficult to collaborate on how you want to spend your time, money, talents, etc., at least there will be no surprises, and over time, and more conversations, the differences may lessen.

26

Passion, Skills & Values

*As you make your transition
into post-career life, one of the biggest factors
is how to use your time.
It is a phase of discovery and exploring options
for an enriched and satisfying life.*

*The following essays are meant to
guide you through this time of discovery
and exploration, helping you to
thoroughly examine who you want to be
and how you want to live at this stage.*

29

7

Blossoms

"And the time came when the risk to remain tight in a bud was more painful than the risk it took to blossom".

— *Anonymous*

What is waiting to blossom in you?

What thought, idea, passion, or dream is waiting to be nourished and opened in you? Are you longing to learn, to write, to design, to teach, to build, to mentor? What will it take to open your self to the risk to blossom? As the bud must have your active participation to give it the particular water, air, light, and food it needs to open and flourish, so does the potential in you.

What will you cultivate?

Within the bud sits the opportunity for your skills, values, passion, interests, education, and learning to - once it blossoms - meet the needs of the world. Whether it is one person, a group of people, a community or beyond, that is the place where both you as giver and the other(s) as receiver will be fed and nourished to cultivate the places where new buds will open and flourish.

What will you do with the yield?

What will you do with the yield from the care and attention it takes to blossom? Where will you take what you have tended and grown so that others may benefit? Is it the classroom, the community, the studio, or a place not yet imagined? How will what you cultivate in yourself and others continue to grow and blossom?

31

Where's the Wonder?

We live in a culture that is focused on getting things done. Busyness is embedded in the routine of our daily lives. Much of what drives our busyness is our 'shoulds'. If our 'shoulds' don't motivate us, we can count on expectations – our own and others' - to get us moving. The art of wonder, abundant in childhood, is all but lost as we hurry through our adult lives.

32

If we wonder at all in the midst of our busyness, we are likely to wonder: "Did I turn off the…before I left?"; "Would he/she/they wait a few more days for…?"; "How long has it been since I called…?"; "Is it time for mom's/dad's/pet's/child's checkup?", and so on.

Then there is the wonder that helps us forget our busyness and routines, the wonder of nature, a concert, an exhibit, or a thought-provoking lecture. Activities that offer us the opportunity to wonder at a deeper level. If we are open to it, we may notice something stirring within. It may sound something like this: "Hmmm, I'd like to know more about...." "Maybe I could take some time to...." "I've always wanted to learn to...."

However, before we can take these stirrings beyond the moment, the realities of life return allowing the 'shoulds' and expectation to drive our lives.

Vacations give us an even wider berth for wonder. But they're over in a blink, and 'shoulds' and expectations quickly come flooding back. This seems a rather bleak existence. Nevertheless this is reality for most of us.

What if the stirrings that began in you during those opportune moments were allowed to continue? The moments when you were moved by the wonder of a beautiful scene, the joy of being in touch with your body through exercise or the warmth of the sun, the wonder in a piece of sculpture, a drawing, or a piece of music shared with a special someone.

What would it take to capture and hold that wonder? What would it look like? What would you do with it?

How would you begin?

Journaling about your thoughts, feelings, surroundings, and senses during or shortly after these experiences is a good way to begin. Reading children's books, spending time with children, recalling and doing some of the things that made you wonder as a child are excellent ways to grab hold of wonder.

Commit to intentionally build wonder into your day so that it becomes the usual rather than the exception. Why? When you include wonder in your day, it may invoke in you a desire to carry it forward. To expand on your wonder and share it with others in ways that can make a difference in your world, in another's world, or within a community.

In addition to wondering about the things you need to get done, what if you made it part of your daily life to include wonder at a deeper level. Wouldn't it be worth a try?

NOTES

35

9

New Times, New Wisdom, New You

Who are the people you turn to when faced with tough choices? When life-changing decisions stop you in your tracks? Who has inspired you in times of doubt or shared timely wisdom when you were most confused?

As you enter this new phase of life and begin to explore new dreams, journeys, and directions, are they the individuals to best advise, guide, and inspire you now? This is a time to evaluate your changing and evolving needs, and to seek the support that best fits those needs.

As you move from full time work, and begin to sort out your options, deciding what to do can be overwhelming. Maybe you will work part time – either in your current field or in something new. Or you may decide to volunteer as a way to express your compassion, or look for an outlet for your creativity, or try on a new career. What advice, counsel, support, and wisdom will you need as you explore your many options?

Begin with knowing yourself. You may not have had the time or inclination in the past, but at this stage of life, it is essential to have a full understanding of who you truly are, what you need, and how you want to use your time. If you are stuck and unsure, it may be time to reach out to new mentors/advisors. Those that can help you take that first step forward and possibly beyond.

Check in with your current mentors/advisors/supporters and share your present needs and goals. Ask if they are willing and able to join you in exploring this new journey. Decide together what makes sense at this juncture, and whether you need to reach out beyond your current circle.

Where do you begin? Think of people you know and whom others know that may be good sources for your current area of need and/or interests. Choose people that have the experience, background, and/or knowledge that fit with your current life phase. People want

37

to help, but you have to ask them, and you have to tell them how to help.

What is the best approach? Begin at the place you presently find yourself. If you primarily want someone to lend an ear and no more, then ask for that. If you want advice or counsel, be specific. Be prepared to ask some questions.

For example:

- What skills do you see in me that would make a good substitute teacher?
- I've always wanted to write, but don't think I would be any good. What would you suggest I do to get past this barrier?
- I want to volunteer but want to give no more than a few hours. How do I learn to say 'no' appropriately?
- What classes would you suggest to enhance my learning in technology?

Wherever you are in your planning, whether you are moving toward your future, or are currently immersed in the joys and fears of the new unknown, seeking new wisdom for new times will help shape the new you.

10

Questions & Answers

*"I would like to beg you dear Sir, as well as I can, to
have patience with everything unresolved in your heart
and to try to love the questions themselves as if they
were locked rooms or books written in a very foreign
language. Don't search for the answers, which could not
be given to you now, because you would not be able to
live them. And the point is to live everything. Live the
questions now. Perhaps then, someday far in the future,
you will gradually, without even noticing it, live your
way into the answer."*

— *Rainer Maria Rilke*

40

Later-life choices for our parents and grandparents were
limited and predictable; their decisions often made for

them, their questions often answered before asked.

Today, our choices for later life are the opposite. We must plan and choose carefully to sustain our quality of life over a much longer period of time. We are faced with questions, to which the answers do not easily fall into a 'one-size-fits all' category.

The task before us may be the most daunting of our lives, as the unknowns far outweigh what is known.

Where do we begin? How do we make the task less daunting? Perhaps, the answer lies in Rainer Maria Rilke's advice. That is, answer the questions that can be answered, and let the remaining questions evolve.

What are your burning questions? Sort out those you can answer quickly, while also giving notice to those that need more research (finances, where to live, health care, etc.). Then allow the remaining questions to 'live' in you. Questions such as:

- ʊ How will I spend my time?
- ʊ How can I find purpose and give meaning to my life?

○ How should I use my strengths, gifts and experience?

○ What are my options? My opportunities?

This requires an openness to exploring all that comes your way, without judgment, with trust, wonder, creativity, vulnerability, and patience!

Allow space for ideas to grow, and give them time to mull. Some will come and go, some will be tossed around and tossed out, and others can be tucked away for a later look. Bring a trusted friend into this place. Someone who will listen and absorb along with you until, at a time you least expect it, you will be rewarded with an "AHA"! AHAs are more likely to show themselves when not pushed and prodded. They come from the whole of you – your past, present, and also your future.

And so I beg you…let your later life decisions evolve from answers that surprise you rather than questions that challenge you.

42

NOTES

43

11

Do You Believe?

Dreams, Goals and Barriers

Self-efficacy, the belief that one's potential can be real-ized, is at the core of successfully choosing a new path, or beginning anything that is filled with a lot of unknowns.

44

Yet, self-efficacy is often overlooked in the process of reaching for and actualizing new dreams and goals. After a lifetime reacting to needs outside ourselves, we grow out of touch with that early, intractable belief in self. I encourage you then, to begin a new life goal by taking a measure of your self-efficacy. Because, If you fail in your heart and soul to **believe** that you can elicit and actualize untried dreams and goals, you may run headlong into a wall of self-made barriers - that which our minds create to lock us in our comfort zone.

Self-made barriers, as such, are easy to miss. They

sound something like this: "What if I fail?"; "I don't have enough money"; "I'm too old!"; "My partner, husband, wife, friends, children, etc. will never support me!"; "So much of my time is needed to help (name)". These laments are easily justified by common sense and logic. But when you operate from your head, it puts you in an *either/or* position and locks you in place. Our minds then, often act as the great gatekeepers that hold our tender hearts and souls from realizing true fulfillment!

Post-career life especially brings with it a particular vulnerability. It may mean you have one chance to really try a new thing. This will involve risks including how you approach personal goals. If in the past, self-made barriers held you back, try a position of **both/and.** How? Recover your belief in self, accept the so-called barriers, deal with them, and move on!

Really Believe

What does it take to believe – really believe – that you can do what you dream of doing?

Some take a reactive approach, and jump in head first.

Others move only when a catalyst gives them permission to move. And still others take the procrastination approach, waiting and waiting for the 'sure thing'. Whatever your approach, begin by going deep inside to see what beliefs no longer work. Mourn them (they served you well at one time), and then release them to make room for the new. Look for ways that work best for you, and proceed slowly. New beliefs are likely to take hold when you are deliberate and intentional. Some things to consider include relying on positive personal history and experience, reality testing, trying on a few things, working with a counselor, a coach, or asking for the support of non-judgmental friends who will keep you accountable and cheer you on.

46

Moving forward

When all is congruent – when mind, heart, and soul are working together, there is a greater chance for self-efficacy to take hold. Your ideas, passions, and dreams will have a chance to move with, and through the inevitable barriers, and restore belief in yourself.

47

12

Growing Up is Hard to Do!

Ask a child, "What do you want to be when you grow up?" and you will get a quick and ready response: an astronaut! A fireman! A pilot! A teacher! And so on. They call out the stuff of dreams without hesitation or restraint. They are firm in the belief that their dreams will come true.

48

Do you remember longing for that grown-up day when your dreams would all come true? You may know one or two people who actually made that happen. But most of us followed a very different and often unexpected path.

Whatever your path, if you still wonder, 'what will I be when I grow up', you're not alone. In my work as a coach, I hear it often. I've been in that place myself.

It usually surfaces in times of transition. When we feel vulnerable, bored, or uncertain about our future. We anxiously seek answers, but answers come less quickly than in the wondrous childhood years.

Yet, we still want quick and easy answers. But, our grown-up, pragmatic, adult selves quickly conjure up past experiences, loaded with embedded beliefs. If our pasts give us any indication that we have limitations, we tend to forget all the good stuff about ourselves, and take the safe route. That helps us keep the status quo, and firmly stuck in our comfort zones. We go with the belief that trying something new will be too difficult and failure is likely. If you resonate with that, how has that belief worked for you?

Well, what if instead, you try a different approach to the *'what-do-I-want-to-be...'* question? Approach it as a child would – without hesitation, without restraint, believing in possibilities. Change must start there. If you can move aside your roadblocks, the first steps will be easier. First steps include the willingness to be open to reflection, feedback, research, discussion, listening, ideas, and embracing 'maybes' and possibilities.

To help you move around your roadblocks, and take the first steps, give some thought to the following questions. As

49

you consider these questions, think about your strengths, your skills, and the value you bring to a new venture.

- ☺ What are the characteristics that you consistently demonstrate in situations where you feel most accomplished?
- ☺ How would you describe your uniqueness and areas of expertise (what do you do that makes you stand out as a person)?
- ☺ How would you describe others' perception of what they can consistently expect from you (your peers, colleagues, clients, customers, friends, family)?

Ask for help from those who know you. How would they answer these questions about you? This process can help you tap into the openness of your child within, and may move you closer to knowing what you really want to be when you grow up. Is it worth a try?

51

13

Becoming Yourself

You are not finished. There's more to be done. You've just begun to be you.

In his book, *Finding Meaning in the Second Half of Life,* James Hollis offers a challenge to those of us approaching and/or living in our second half of life. He writes:

"In this new century, we have twice the length of adult life than our forebears were granted. Thus we are faced with an unprecedented opportunity and responsibility to live more consciously…. We may wonder, 'Since I have served the expectations of my culture, reproduced my species, become a socially productive citizen and taxpayer, what now?' What in short, is the second half of life about…if it is not to repeat the script and expectations of the first half of life?"

Good question!

As Hollis contends, our old scripts were pretty much written for us. Now, with the freedom to write our own, where do we begin without the cultural/societal compass that has guided us in the past?

At this stage, we have our life experience and some notion of our capabilities to build on and to guide us. However, after a lifetime of striving to meet pre-scripted expectations, we are conditioned to focus outside of ourselves.

With an outward focus, we tend to live more reactively than proactively. Our actions are less likely to be based on what we want, and more on what others want from us or for us. An inward focus helps us to know and better understand ourselves. It gives us a chance to think and feel before we act.

With an over-developed ability to focus outward, the task then is to also develop our inward focus. How do we make the shift to cultivate an inward focus?

Begin with what you know for sure: your gender, age, roles, and life experience. Move on to noting your strengths and weaknesses, your likes and dislikes, how you like to spend your time, and what you value. Then, think about your talents, dreams, and passions. Be prepared to notice what stops you as you venture away from old scripts and expectations. What thoughts, emotions, voices (yours and others) deny you a new life script? It's helpful to pay attention to them, but only as a way to sort out what is useful or not.

Once your inward focus is developed to balance your outward focus, you will find that you can more proactively weigh your decisions and choices and act from a place of authenticity. This will serve you well in the second half of life - a time to honor, respect, and loyally dissect the parts that are you. It's a time to keep what you want, and discard the rest.

Self-examination is the key to writing your new life scripts. You may find that using an inward/outward focus takes a path where your authentic self is mined for the good of both yourself and others.

I have witnessed the culmination of this process in colleagues and friends. One uses her gifts of knitting, creating beauty, and generating compassion by making shawls for the families of abuse victims. I've seen it in my lawyer friend, who took time to become a Master Gardener, caring for and beautifying the earth. Another friend has prepared for her next stage of life by training to be a specialized yoga teacher, using her gifts and passion for teaching and serving others.

It takes courage to stand up and profess your authenticity. It can be painful and exhilarating, supported and criticized.

Yet, there is also freedom in accepting yourself as a work in progress. One who is not yet finished, and is willing to discard the scripts that no longer work, and to take the risk to become oneself.

14

Being of Service:
Make it a win/win

"Our deepest calling is to grow into our own authentic self-hood, whether or not it conforms to some image of who we ought to be. As we do so, we will not only find the joy that every human being seeks--we will also find our path of authentic service in the world."

— *Parker J. Palmer*

56

Being of service brings to mind the volunteering of time and talents to help another, a cause, or a mission, while also contributing to a greater good. It is a noble and necessary way to serve and is highly regarded in our culture and society.

Opportunities to serve as a volunteer are limitless, often making it difficult to choose the 'best' or 'right' way to serve. Volunteering can bring not only a good feeling, but also a sense of guilt if we think we aren't doing enough. Our jobs and careers leave us little time to give back. We look to retirement as a time to give more of ourselves.

Yet, when the time comes, volunteering may feel more like a 'should' than a 'want'. Service and volunteering are often seen as two sides of one coin. Yet in reality, volunteering is just one way to serve. Service is multifaceted. One can serve without pay, with pay, or a combination of the two. The key is to think of serving as a 'want to' (a choice). So much of your adult life is based on assumptions of what you 'should' do or 'have to' do. As you move toward and into retirement, think in terms of choice.

Choosing how you want to serve is easier if you think of it as a proactive process – one that includes thought, creativity, research, trial and error, self-exploration, and discovery. It is likely that you will find greater fulfillment in your post-career life, if you use a proactive approach. Think of it as a personal project to give and receive good, and proceed in a framework of choice. What you do, how and when you do it is up to YOU.

Not to suggest that you make such decisions in a vacuum. Those who are impacted by your choices must be included. Ask and answer the questions that pop up. For example, will you need to be paid? If so, how much? How do you want to spend your days? What will you need to feel fulfilled? Who can benefit from your service? What do you want to learn, and how will you apply what you learn?

Weigh all the factors – health, relationships, leisure, work, learning, financial, personal growth, fulfillment - and serve in the ways that make sense for YOUR life.

Whether you serve for pay, without pay, or a combination, when you use a proactive approach, having evaluated all the necessary factors, service becomes an authentic giving and receiving for the good of all involved. A win/win.

15

Legacy of Character

As organizations face a huge loss of talented workers to retirement, the need to capture corporate knowledge prior to that loss is both a great challenge and a necessity for the continued success of the organization.

For those in leadership positions, leaving an organization is no longer just a matter of packing one's belongings and moving on. Human resources across organizations are increasingly asked to prepare leadership succession plans – plans that in the past have been equated primarily with family-owned businesses. It's a way to ensure that sources of information found in best practices, lessons learned, and personal wisdom, are not lost.

New sources of talent are sought internally and externally to carry these competencies forward.

Gifts of character add value as well. This task, however,

falls to individuals to first recognize their own qualities, and then to make the value of character apparent through mentorships, supervision, and people management

What about you? Do you recognize– beyond your job description - the combination of knowledge, wisdom, experience, personality, and talents that make up your character? What is it that sets you apart from your peers or colleagues? In large part, it is likely something innate in you. Something that if asked, you may wonder, "Doesn't everyone do that?"

Consider what you want to import to other employees. What characteristics do you hope others will carry on in your place? Will find important to do? Will remember to do? For example: are you someone who readily offers an unsolicited compliment? Or steps in to lighten another's load without being asked? Do you bring levity during times of tension, or give recognition or gratitude when unexpected? Do you have a talent for giving difficult feedback or hard news in a caring, constructive manner? Are you a good listener? Do people feel heard and understood by you? Are honesty and integrity values that you invoke in others by way of example? You may not recognize your own qualities. You may not realize the impact you have had. I suggest you ask others who have worked closely with you. How would they describe your contributions of character?

The legacy of character you leave to the workplace can also transfer to your personal legacy. As you transition to post-career life, which of your characteristics do you want others to learn from, emulate, and carry forward? Not only those closest to you, but also anyone you spend time with in part-time work, as a volunteer, with new friends and acquaintances, etc.

Rather than passively moving on to your next life phase, thinking about your post-career life in this way offers an intentional and proactive approach to a richer experience, while also giving you time to reflect on what you value most in terms of making a difference in those who follow you.

Intention, Goals, Action
& Barriers

Following the process of exploration,

discovery and reflection, comes the time to

set goals, plan, and take action.

This can be the most difficult part of the process,

as it means moving into unknown territory.

That, and the time we have to

bring our lives to fulfillment

is likely the shortest we've encountered.

The following essays are meant to

empower you to go forward with intention,

goals, and actions that fit with the life

you wish to lead, while also working with

the certainty of barriers

you will meet along the way.

16

Plan Your Life With Intention

When the phase of life commonly known as retirement approaches, a number of questions pop up. Primarily, pre-retirees want to know, "What are my options?"

Once their financial questions are addressed: "How much do I have? " and "How much will I need?" they want to know: "How will I spend my time?" This pattern follows the theory of renowned psychologist Abraham Maslow who maintained that our need for food, shelter, and security must be met before we can focus on relationships, followed by self-esteem and, finally, self-actualization.

Collectively, these are new issues for today's retirees as they have many more options than previous generations.

After living out the expectations of a society that offered lock-step answers for each phase of life (i.e., college, jobs, careers, home investment, raising families, etc.), Baby Boomers especially feel ill equipped to make decisions for a future that is less defined.

Because you want to make the most of this time, you want quick answers. My suggestion is to slow down, take a step back, and pose a different kind of question. That is, "What is my intention?" This exercise can help you identify, narrow, and choose options that make sense for you and your life. Write your answer quickly without a lot of thought or analysis. This will allow your emotions to speak first and to get to the heart of what is most important.

For example, I tried this exercise and discovered that, while my intention is to allow a significant amount of time to write and coach, I was surprised that I quickly wrote: "To keep my financial pump primed." Financial solvency came first, and how to get it done – through my writing and coaching - was second. Both are important to me, but until I tried this exercise, I didn't realize that financial solvency was at the heart of my choices and required the more immediate focus. This gave me key criteria for prioritizing my actions to continue what I love to do! Rather than having a "build it and they will come" attitude, the wisdom of having a plan was reinforced in me.

Declaring your intention can help you get to the next step: identifying options that fit with your intention. If, for example, your intention is 'to feel useful for as long as possible', begin with your definition of 'useful'. What does 'feeling useful' mean to you? Is it *helping others?* If so, what population do you want to help most, and in what way? Will you need to receive pay or volunteer your services? What strengths do you want to use and/ or learn, and what values are important to you?

This exercise will be easy for some, difficult for others. One way to facilitate the process is to quickly write your intention, share it with a trusted friend or colleague, and ask for feedback. If you find it difficult to begin, once again a friend or colleague may help, or you may turn to a coach or mentor, depending on what you have at stake.

Once you determine your key criteria for this phase of life, you have more information from which to seek options or to narrow options already considered. Depending on who you are, your intention and follow-on actions will be distinctive. Having too many options, or not knowing what they are, can act as barriers to taking action. When you quickly write the answer to "What is my intention?" and address the questions that are sure to follow, you will have a great start to planning your life with intention.

17

Slow Forward

Are you at a threshold – a place of options and choices, where decisions are waiting to be made?

Each of us has our own approach to decision-making. It depends on our investment in the outcome and how it impacts our lives. Typical approaches include: readily moving forward; moving neither forward nor backward; or turning back. Whatever your process, and no matter what is at stake, it's important to make your decisions with intention, to take your time, and to develop a plan.

Plans help us stay front and center in our lives. As organizations find it difficult to succeed without plans, it can be equally difficult for individuals if they don't know where they're going, or how they will get there.

Leaders use strategy to project the successful future of their organizations. It begins with a plan that identifies

70

the values of the organization (what is important to us?). Next, the vision for the future is evaluated (where do we want to be; what do we want to do?), and finally, a mission is developed (what do we need to do to get there?). The strategy that leaders use to grow their organizations can also help you create a direction for your future.

What is important to you? *(Values)*

What are the principles or standards that you must have for a satisfying lifestyle? It is essential that you identify values that are uniquely yours and not what SHOULD be important to you, or what others may think is important for you. Narrow your values to five or six that are core to your life. This will help you lay a foundation from which to operate authentically. As you create your vision and mission, your core values will be the place to which you can return to ensure that you remain focused.

Where do you want to be; what do you want to do? *(Vision)*

What do you want to accomplish? What are your aspirations? What outcome would you like to have? What is your timeframe?

What do you need to get there? *(Mission)*

What will it take to get you where you want to be? What do you need to equip you? What resources will you need? What support?

What do you want to accomplish, and how will you do it? *(Goals and Actions)*

After identifying your core values, and creating your vision and mission, you will be ready to write your goals, followed by action steps. The key is to set goals that are both manageable AND that will stretch your comfort zone. They can be short-term or long-term, and must be specific and measurable.

Barriers

The final step is to include and plan for barriers that are likely to hold you back. Barriers can include:

- Ourselves (doubt, fear, making time, feeling 'selfish')
- Others ("Are you sure…?"; "You've tried that before…!"; "Have you thought about…?")

Barriers can pop up at any point in the creation of your plan. Name the barriers now that are sure to get in your way. Next, plan ahead for how you will deal with them.

Setting goals, and handling the barriers that may get in your way can be difficult to handle alone. Who do you trust to partner with you in your planning process? Is there one person, or do you prefer to have a few people? Who are they? How can they help?

Identify them and go ask them. They will be honored.

18

Desire, Intention & Action

Life is composed of a complexity of stops, starts, surprises, and sameness. In our natural state, we react to
life's complexities declaring our desire and intention to
create balance, remove stress and find purpose and meaning. As these desires become seemingly inaccessible, our
intention turns from 'I want' to 'I should' or 'I have to'.

74

Acting on intention is difficult for many, as day-to-
day living takes so much energy. We allow internal and
external barriers to get in the way of what we say we want,
and spend energy on being unhappy about not having it.
All the while, our lives are shifting and moving through
different stages. We go to school, secure jobs, make career
decisions, form romantic partnerships, create families,
taking on more and more responsibility. We win, we
lose, we gain, we slip back – literally and emotionally.

The people and circumstances change, but our patterns for how we operate often remain unchanged.

We rarely stop to dream much less take time to make our dreams come true. That is, the dreams we had at the ages of 10 or 12. Ages when our hopes and aspirations had no boundaries; before we became influenced by overt and covert messages from our environment and society, leading us down different paths.

Purpose and meaning may now seem elusive, depending on your 'grownup' version of what is possible. Really, you don't have to wait for the one 'Big Thing' to draw you out, or wait for some future date to focus on making your life meaningful. Think of all that you do now.

What are the things that, when you are doing them, you feel most like your natural self? It may be in your home, in your work, in your community, with friends or family, or in your leisure time. Look at your past. What were the things you did that gave you the greatest pleasure? What in the present gives you meaning? If you look, you can find pieces in every day life that can be constructed into a whole that gives greater meaning and purpose now, and can expand into your future. A future planned with intention, followed by action.

Do you like to write? Do you love to learn? Does mentoring or coaching others give you great satisfaction? Do you find joy in creating a piece of art? Did you change your major in college because you were told that you couldn't earn a living in your chosen field? Is your chosen field, or some form of it still open to you? Take steps to incorporate more of what you love into your current life. Take stock, choose one of your joyful activities, do more of it, or do it more often, or do it because it is something you have always wanted to do.

Confide in someone close to you, or find a mentor or life coach to help you take your ideas beyond your dreams and into action. Most importantly, choose someone you trust who will cheer you on and keep you accountable.

Wherever you are in life, it's possible to transform desire to a declaration of intention, and take action to create opportunity.

77

19

Barriers to Becoming Uniquely You!

How do you express your uniqueness? In what way are you and your gifts like no other? Do you know? Is this the time to go deep, to take stock, to take a close look at your gifts, your strengths? The combination of all that you are makes you unique. There is not another person who is exactly like you. Are you ready to claim this?

Claiming your uniqueness takes courage, as you must be ready to shed the pretenses that you've built around your persona, and to reveal – to yourself and others - who you really are. There is first an excitement around shedding the old, followed by a feeling of vulnerability and exposure. This is the place where barriers will pop up and hold you back, creating indecisiveness and stripping you of your courage to step out and try something new.

The barrier that most often gets in our way is the perceived judgment of others. We may perceive correctly, but it is likely that most of our perceptions are based on thoughts we make up. Our made-up thoughts help us stay safe and secure in our 'known' worlds. We begin to question our audacity to think we could move into an unknown place. We are likely to confront ourselves with questions and convictions that are sure to move us back to safety. It is a creative gesture learned over time until it becomes so familiar, it is difficult to stop and try a new direction.

One way to change direction away from old, unproductive patterns is to listen for the words that pop into your head. Are they focused on assumptions or on reality? Heighten your awareness. Be on the alert. Notice when your thoughts, actions, and words move you forward, and when they lead you away from your goals, desires, and/or purpose. Keep track of them in a journal. After awhile you will see a pattern. What messages keep you from operating from your unique self? Which ones help you step out in courage? This discovery can help you decide which messages to hold on to, and which to weed out.

This is not an easy task and can't be accomplished overnight. Old patterns do not want to let go! Their mission is to serve and protect us from moving out of our comfort zone. It is up to us to discern when to stretch out – when we and others are better served by our unique gifts.

It can be to your great advantage to get support, as surrendering to change is both a backward and forward process. Consider partnering with someone who can help you gain momentum towards embracing the person that is uniquely you!

20

Connections

Once you have made your peace with change and transition, discovered your uniqueness, uncovered your passions, explored your options, and set your intention and goals for your future, think about and include the people places and things to which you have strong connections.

Our social, emotional, and spiritual connections give us a sense of stability, belonging, and purpose, contributing to our ability to stay resilient through the ups and downs of life.

We rely on our connections across the span of our lives. As we go through change, our needs change, and our connections also change. The key sources remain, but what and who they are, take on different faces, names, and meaning.

They include:

- ♂ families
- ♂ friends
- ♂ community networks
- ♂ churches/synagogues/mosques
- ♂ leisure/recreation
- ♂ social relationships
- ♂ learning
- ♂ climate
- ♂ culture
- ♂ health care
- ♂ residence (type and location)

As you look at the list above, take a moment to think about your own sources of connection and circle those that currently serve and add meaning to your life.

Look at them collectively and individually. Unbundle them, and take time to fully reflect on what it is about these people, places, and things that give you a sense of stability, belonging, and/or purpose, and that make you a better person because they exist. Rank them according to the role they currently play in your life. Reflect on these connections and their order of importance. Do they match your needs and align with your choices and decisions for your post-career life?

For example, if you decide to move away from your home base indefinitely or for long periods of time, how will you adjust as you disconnect from these emotional ties? If you think about and plan for this in advance of a move, it can help you disconnect and reconnect gradually and in new ways. You may make different decisions as a result of pre-planning.

The special meaning and connection you have with your sources are unique to you and are likely to be different from those of your spouse, partner, or others who are impacted by your life. They will each have connections that are meaningful to them. Ask them to try the exercise as well and compare. Make your plans to include what is important to each of you, working toward collaboration for a quality of life that fits for both or all.

If, in these essays, you have found inspiration
for any part of your life, I hope you
will share it with me, and with others who may also be
seeking inspiration along this new path of life formerly
known as retirement.

It has been a privilege for me to imagine
you at times flipping through the pages,
at others, stopping to reflect, and perhaps at others
to silently or loudly shout an AHA!

I wish you the best of all that you are,
whether you have always operated
from your 25-year-old self, or have rekindled
that part of you that's been waiting
for your return – the time is now.
Be kind and gentle, accepting and patient
with yourself, and always – be real!

Donna Bennett

Made in the USA
Lexington, KY
14 September 2015